HOW TO MAKE MONEY ONLINE

100 ATTEMPTED and PROVEN ways to making money online! Build an EMPIRE! (Make Money from home, secrets to easy money, passive income, residual income)

By Dimitrius Malary

Table of Contents

66. Guest Posting
67. Selling Music
68. Kickstarter
69. Online Casino
70. Cash Crate
71. Peer to Peer Lending
72. InfoBarrel
73. Squidoo
74. Hubpages
75. Bukisa
76. SheToldMe
77. Best Reviewer
78. Rate It All
79. UpHype
80. Dollar3
81. Fittytown
82. TenBux
83. Facebook Ads
84. Speedy Ads
85. Just Answer
86. Kgb
87. Fun Advice
88. ChaCha
89. Web Answers
90. Gazelle
91. Amazon
92. Shopit
93. Sell.com
94. Oodle
95. Backpage
96. Amazon Associates
97. Commission Junction
98. E-Junkie
99. Cafe Press

100.   <u>E*Trade</u>

Introduction

The American Dream! Financial Freedom! Passive income!

These are the powerful terms that we aim for, seek, work long nights for, pray to our gods for and thrive for as humans. Why is it so hard to attain this goal??

Knowledge is a powerful thing, but the ability to use that knowledge and incorporate it in your daily life is even more powerful! The reason it's so hard to reach this goal is because of the lack of knowledge/research, non-persistence and the fear that derives from lack of self-worth.

There is no limit to your success, as you probably heard before, but it is definitely true. People interpret that statement however they feel. The truth is if you have a vision or goal and you truly desire accomplishing it then you'll work hard enough to make it happen because it is attainable. There is no easy route to getting rich, I would just be pitching a complete lie, well, unless of course you inherited it.

Before you dive into this book, I want to share my motives for creating this piece of work. Some of you, just like I was, may be at the brink of frustration, yearning for financial freedom, tired of having to work a 9-5, or are really interested in making money online and just don't know where to start. Trust me when I say I understand, people all around are at one of these points in their lives and are really thriving for a breakthrough. Fortunately, you don't have to be lost or frustrated anymore because I have provided a blueprint to multiple ways of becoming successful in the making money online niche.

In my eBook, you are going to find out great and effective ways to earn cash from working online. This book covers general descriptions all the way to specifics on noteworthy websites and companies. Use these resources and secrets as a referral to money making strategies that will change your life! Armed with this list, you will be able to begin working from home and tell that bossy boss to kick rocks. Don't waste more time that could be spent using these methods to bring you the life you've always dreamed of!!

Write Product Reviews

There are an ample amount of sites that offer you a way to earn money by writing product reviews for companies. The reviews can be anything from websites all the way to small, physical products. There are many sites that offer this service. One of the top sites is Vandale, but here is a list of different site that you are able to use.

- SponsoredReviews.com
- BuyBlogReviews.com
- ReviewMe.com
- ReviewStream.com
- Paid2Review.co.uk
- ReviewsArena.com
- SurveysPaid.com
- SharedReviews.com
- Vindale.com
- LinkFromBlog.com
- ReviewParty.com
- WriterMag.com
- CarrotReviews.com
- PostsGenius.com
- SoftwareJudge.com
- DailyScrubaDiving.com
- PaidCasinoReviews.co.uk

Sell Books

If you are a bookworm, then you have everything at your fingertips to start selling books online. Every bookworm has books stored somewhere, whether it is on bookshelves, basement, or their garage. If you want to start a nice business that you enjoy, you can begin selling used books online. Begin by going through your own stash and making some choices on which ones to sell. The great thing is you can replenish your used book stash by visiting the shops, yard sale, and more to collect books. You can read them, then sell them.

Online Reward Sites

Just like big credit card businesses reward you with getting cash back, there are many sites that do about the same thing. These sites are known as Get Paid To sites, also known as GPT. These types of sites offer different ways on how to earn the points. You are able to take surveys, answer poll questions, quizzes, games, signing up to different newsletters, checking out websites, and more. Here are some sites that have been established and are trustworthy.

- Swagbucks
- Amazon
- Cashcrate
- Gifthulk
- CashDazzle
- QuickRewards
- CreationRewards

Get Money for Reading Emails

Yes, you can even earn money reading emails. The way that it works is advertisers will pay different sites like InboxDollars to help send traffic to their websites. As a reward for visiting the websites, the managing site will offer shares in some of the advertising dollars that are paid to them for the traffic.

They will send emails to you and it will be promoting a certain service or product. You will then click on the contained ink inside of the email, the account holder will get the credit. It does not even matter if you have made a purchase on the advertiser's site, just as long as you clicked the link. Here are a few of the sites:

- Inbox Dollars
- SendEarning
- Cash4Offers
- InboxPays

Start A Blog

A blog is a very easy way to start earning money, and it can also be free. Once you have picked something you would like to write about, then you can build your blog. Make it look nice and ensure that it matches your niche. For example, you would not write a blog on flowers and use skyscrapers as a theme. After you have written some posts, then it would be time for you to monetize it. Here is a list of websites you can use to ensure that you make money from it.

- Google Adsense
- Affiliate Links
- Pay Per Post Sites
- Sponsored Reviews
- Linkworth
- SocialSpark

Free Blogging Platforms:
- Blogger
- WordPress
- LiveJournal
- Blog.com
- Tumblr

Smartphone Apps

The popularity of apps has been exploding over the years. There are virtually thousands of apps available that make it very easy for you to spend money on shopping, there are some that will help you make some money though too. Here are some phone apps that you are able to use to earn money:

- *Gigwalk*: This is a mobile marketplace. This is on Apple and Android in order to perform simple field work that is required, these can include mystery shopping, testing apps, delivering items, taking pictures, and more.
- Field Agent: This is close to how Gigwalk works. Users use scan bars, check prices, mystery shop, talk polls, and more. This is available on iPhone.
- *Shopkick*: This is an app that pays for shopping trips. You can be paid in points to use for gift cards and discounts. The app works for Androids and iPhones.
- *Check Points*: This company rewards their users with points and other rewards for scanning products, playing games, completing different
- *Easy Shift*: This is a phone app that works like Gigwalk. There are different jobs like taking pictures, recording different prices, and more. You can get paid from $2 up to $20 per job.
- *Apptrailers*: You can earn points from just watching videos and downloading apps. You can turn in your rewards for gift cards.

Answer Questions and Give Advice

There are different sites that will offer you pay for answering questions and giving advice to those that ask for it. It can be as simple as how to train a puppy up to how to find advice about legal issues. Sites like this include:

- SmallBiz Advice
- Keen
- WerLive
- Ammas
- ChaCha
- JustAnswer

Freelancing

One of the most known ways to earn money online is to freelance. You can do it from your own home or from the local free Wi-Fi spot. The great thing about becoming a freelancer is that you do not need any money to start, only a bit of time. There are different sites that you are able to sell your skills on in order to make some money.

- oDesk
- Freelancer
- PeoplePerHour
- 99Designs
- Guru
- iFreelance

Write Articles

Writing articles can be an amazing way to earn some money. The internet is made of websites, and the sites are content. This means that there will be a demand for writers for years to come. Here are some sites that can be utilized to fill your bank account.

- Constant Content
- Textbroker
- Cracked
- Seeking Alpha
- Fool
- Postloop
- DemandStudios

Paid to Click

This type of way to make money can be a bit tedious, yet it does pay out. You can even refer other people to make more money. For every click you make, you will make a small little profit. A couple of the sites that you can use like this are:

- Neobux
- Clixsense

Affiliate Marketing

This is a wonderful way to make money. There are people doing this on a daily basis, and those who put a lot of effort into their beginning have ended up quitting their jobs and working from home. This is where you advertise products from companies and you get a percentage of every sell that you send their way. Here are some companies that offer affiliate programs:

- Amazon Associates
- eBay Partner Network
- Commission Junction
- MaxBounty
- ClickBank

Micro Jobs

There are many micro job sites popping up. One of the biggest micro job site that is more known now is Fiverr. This is a bit like freelancing gigs; however, you get to offer your skills for a specified price. Those who need your skill will hire you and pay you the fee you requested at the beginning. Here are a few sites to use:

- Fiverr
- mTurk
- Microworkers
- ClickChores

Revenue Sharing

Revenue sharing is a smart concept in which companies use. You will sign up as a member, publish your content like articles, eBooks, videos, etc, and then you will share your advertising fees with the companies. There are some sites that will split the profit of the advertising dollars to which you would get 70 percent, and there are some that offer 95 percent. Here are a few of the sites that you can use:

- Hubpages
- Squidoo
- InfoBarrel
- WebAnswers

Market Research

There are businesses that are always searching for ideas that will help improve their business or their product. If you are a part of a certain demographic or live in a certain area, you may match up to the specifics for market research. A good site to use is 2020 Panel. You can help companies with products like:

- Clothing
- Food Products
- Personal Products

Sell Designs

Thanks to today's technology, you are able to use sites to sell your designs to anyone that loves them or needs them. All you have to do is just become a member of a sites. There are many people that design cool pictures and sell them for bags, mugs, towels, and so much more. Here are some sites that you can use to sell your unique designs:

- Cafepress
- Etsy
- Skreend
- SpreadShirt
- PrintFection
- Zazzle

Stock Photography

If you are an amateur or professional photographer, then you will be happy to know that you are able to sell the rights to use your pictures to individuals and companies. They will be able to use your work in projects ranging from films to websites. There are stipulations to using your art, like crediting you on their site. There are different guidelines that you can set for you work depending on the site that you use. Here is a list of sites that can offer you a way to sell your photography:

- ShutterStock
- iStockPhoto
- DreamsTime
- BigStockPhoto
- Crestock
- PhotoStockPlus
- 123RoyaltyFree
- Fotolia
- ShutterPoint
- StockXpert

Tweet for Money

This one you will have to build your Twitter account up for. There are many companies that will pay you to tweet to your followers, but in order for it to be worth the advertising dollars, you will have to have thousands of followers, not the typical hundreds. It is proved that consumers will purchase a product from someone on their social media accounts, rather than a company ad that is strategically placed in a Google search. Here are some sites that you can use to get matched up with to earn money from tweets:

- SponsoredTweets
- PaidPerTweet
- Twivert
- TwitPub

Sell New and Used Items

If you have a stockpile of items that you do not really need or items that you want to get rid of, yet do not want to throw away, then selling them online is the best idea. This will offer you a way to make money off of items that are just sitting around. If you would like to grow a small little business out of it, you can utilize thrift stores and other resale shops to purchase inventory to resell. Some sites include:

- Craigslist
- eBay
- Gazelle
- Backpage
- Amazon

Paid Surveys

Just like focus groups, there are online surveys that are used to conduct research on the behalf of companies and manufacturers. This offers them feedback from the consumers in order to tune in their product or their service. Some sites include:

- MySurvey
- Survey Spot
- GlobalTestMarket
- iSurveyWorld
- PineCone Research

Online Games

Before you get excited, you have to understand these games do not include XBox360 or Playstation. These games include those that are online. Here are some website that you can use to earn cash and have some fun.

- CashDazzle
- LalaLoot
- Swagbucks
- GSN
- Exodus3000
- SecondLife

Website Flipping

Think of house flipping. People purchase a home, fix it up, and then they sell it for more. Same thing applies here. You will purchase a domain name, build a functioning site, and then you will sell it to someone who likes it. They will then take over the site and you will no longer have anything to do with the site other than enjoying the money you received from it. Sites that you can build and then flip include those related to:

- Parenting
- Football
- Fishing
- Beauty
- Making Money

Buy and Sell Domain Names

This is a very effective way to put some extra cash in your pocket. All there is to it is thinking of clever domains that people would like to buy for companies and other hobbies. Once you have purchased these domain names, you can then sell them off for a good price that will put money in the bank.

Blog Flipping

This is just like website flipping only you will do this with a blog. You will build a blog and then add posts to it. Once you have built up a blog with content and a good amount of traffic, you will then put it on the market. Someone who is interested in this blog will purchase the blog and continue with its success. You can build blogs around these ideas:

- Parenting
- Beauty
- Movie
- Fishing
- Basketball
- Make-Up

Write and Sell eBooks

If you enjoy writing, then you are able to make a living at it if you decide that you would like to become an author. No matter what you like to write, whether it is non-fiction, fiction, guide, etc. You can write eBooks and sell them on Amazon or Kindle. Ideas for eBook types:

- Non-Fiction
- Fiction
- How to Guides
- Cook Books
- Children Books

Ghost Write

There are those who want to make a name for him or herself as a writer, yet do not have time to do it. You can write their vision for them for a fee and they can put their name on it. Often time this is non-fiction work and requires research skills, which is a fun part of the job. Here are subjects that clients need when hiring a ghostwriter.

- Cook Books
- Non-Fiction
- Children Books

Forum Poster

There are companies that will pay those that have the time to post to forums. This keeps conversation going. Most companies and websites do this in order to keep their websites popping up on search results and to keep traffic coming back. It can be a fun job is you decide that you want to post on a site that has a subject that you are interested in.

Edit a Blog

There are many different blogs that need a full time or a part time person to help keep things up to date. The editor will make a list of good article subjects, go through articles already posted, and other types of maintaining the blog. This can be a fun and relaxing way to make some money, especially if you are working on a blog that you are interested in.

Edit Writing

Many blogs, forums, and ghostwriters need an editor. What this entails is going through different types of writing pieces and editing them for grammar, spelling, and other types of mistakes. You will be the last person to read the piece before publication. You help the writer tweak the piece until it is perfect. A great position as an editor would be a partnership with a person that writes eBooks as a living.

Technical Writer

A technical writer is a writer that produces technical documentation that will help people better understand a service or product. This document will include manuals, online help, and more. There are many different companies that need this type of writing so that their consumers are able to use their product in the correct manner. This type of writing can be hard, yet fun at times.

Copy Editing

Copywriting is content that is written and is conveyed using online media, as well as printed materials. This is typically content that helps companies advertising materials. It can contain press releases, blurbs, and more. There are so many people that work directly with companies themselves, and they work from home earning a good-sized paycheck.

Comment on Blogs

In order for a blog to stay registered in the search engine, it has to be kept going with continuous activity, and this means the blog needs people to comment on it. It will also encourage other people to interact with the blog, and thus will also drive traffic.

Be an eTutor

If you are an expert on any subject, then you can become an eTutor. These tutors will help teach other people about the subject of their profession. There are also teachers that moonlight on different website to help children and teens gain control over their academics. There is decent money in tutoring online and location does not matter since it is over the internet.

Write Paid Reviews

Many companies will offer you money to write reviews about their services or their products. This will help create brand awareness and increase their sells. This will offer you a great way to make money while staying at home. You can contact companies, or you can get connected through different websites.

Donation Links

If you run a website or a blog, then you can put a link for donations on your site. If people have a few bucks and use your site a lot, then they will send it to you. All you will need is a PayPal account hooked up to your link and you can receive the money.

Private Ad Spots

Once you get a blog or a website up and going, you will need to build up traffic. These numbers will be important. After the traffic is steady, you can sell certain spots on your website or your blog to advertisers for one month, three months, six months, and in year increments. If you have multiple pages, then you have many different opportunities to earn a large amount of money through this type of passive income.

Develop and Sell Wordpress Plugins

The typical website designer knows how important plugins are to their work. Without plugins, there would be no interacting with most websites. If you are familiar with building plugins, then building a few plugins and selling them through Wordpress is a great idea. It is a renewable product that you will only have to do once to continuously earn money.

Build and Sell Templates

Templates are crucial to many different aspects of businesses and for individuals. Building templates takes up a lot of time depending on familiarity and how fast you work. This being said, you can make passive income off of one design you put a lot of effort into. Starting from Excel templates all the way to theme templates for web design, there are many needs for the templates. This is a great way to earn money. Examples are:

- Theme Forest
- Templamatic
- BuyStockDesign

Design eBook Covers

The sale of eBooks is rapidly increasing, and so is the need for eBook covers. Although there are many writers out there spending time on the actual book, yet they need covers designed. You will build a reputation very fast if you jump in and start designing cover after cover. Design a few mock-ups to show them what you can do.

Develop and Sell Android and iPhone Apps

With the growth of smartphones being used as tiny computers, apps are going crazy. From apps that offer you a way of typing or tracking money all the way to apps that offer continuous music play and games, there is virtually no way you could not come up with an idea for many different apps. Think of one and jump in. Sell it in the iPhone and the Android store.

Setup Blogs

There are many people who want to start a blog, yet do not have the capability or the time to set up their blog. They will hire you to set up and maintain their blog. You will work with the blog owner on the theme and other aspects of the blog to offer a great visual blog. Here are the steps that you will take:

- Make a domain name.
- Build the blog.
- Design the theme.

Design Websites

There are many business and individuals that want to build a site, but they do not know how. There are many different aspects that go into designing websites from user-friendly interfaces all the way to how the blog elements are displayed. You will be able to design websites to the owner's specifications for a good amount of money. From mechanic shops all the way to flower boutiques, they need your help.

Design Banners

Many entrepreneurs, companies, businesses, and more look for those who can build virtual banners. These banners are a marketing tool for those people to aid in their success. Have you seen the banners on websites? Those are a great way to build up your money. Designing these takes time and attention. You are able to build the banners and websites for authors, companies, specific products, and more.

Design Logos

Logos are an important aspect of having a business. They help create brand awareness. Many companies need a new design or a new logo design. This is a good way for some money-making opportunities. Typically a logo designer will do three different designs in order to offer choices for the company that needs the logo. This is a creative and fun job.

Social Media Marketing

Social media marketing is important for any business. This drives traffic to their sites, and then turns into sales. You can offer your time for this. Typically the marketer will get paid an hourly wage for this. They will post on their social media platforms in order to gain company awareness for those that have hired them. Sites that you can utilize for this purpose include:

- Twitter
- Google
- Facebook
- MySpace
- Tumblr

Search Engine Optimization Services

Search engine optimization helps drive traffic to a websites. Typically a person is hired to go through website content to ensure that the content on the website is SEO friendly. This means that there are appropriate SEO measures taken to keep the traffic coming. From titles to the body of the content, SEO is important when a person is looking for a product or services your client provides.

Link Building Services

Link building is the process of establishing inbound links to a specific website. This will help companies bring in more traffic. This is done by adding the website link in comments, guests posts, social media posts, and more. Those who do the link building normally get a flat fee or can get an hourly wage.

Forum Moderator

Forums are still used tremendously. There can be bullies, spam, and other information and content that does not belong on a specific forum or in a thread. The forum normally has a forum moderator to ensure the quality of the forum stays high and the spam stays out. There are guidelines to every forum and the moderator ensures that people follow them.

Virtual Assistant

A virtual assistant position is widely known since the boom of the internet. People work online and now with this a position has been created for those working from home to aid with business. A virtual assistant will take phone calls, do research, answer emails, and more. This position is important to those who run online businesses and those who work through the internet for many business purposes. Virtual assistants receive an hourly wage.

Reseller Hosting

Reseller hosting is a type of web hosting where the account owner will use his or her hard drive for space, along with bandwidth to host other websites for third parties. The reseller will buy the host services on wholesale, and then they will sell them to their own customers for a profit.

Online Data Entry

This is a position in which a person transcribes information into another type of medium It is done through a computer program. There are forms of data that is used by people and companies like handwritten documents into spreadsheets, and more. These people will normally get paid per project. If you are a fast typer, then you may like this relaxed position.

Transcription Jobs

There are many different companies that look for people to transcribe documents into another language. From documents to eBooks, you will take one form of the document and then rewrite it into another language. There are many movie sites that hire those that are bilingual to write subtitles in another language so that they can offer their movies to other countries.

Sell Items on eBay

Selling items on eBay can drastically improve your cash flow. From used items to custom made decor, there is virtually no end to what you can sell on eBay. There are many people who purchase bulk items and then resell them individually on eBay for a good profit. For example, if you were to purchase ten pairs of high end jeans for only five dollar a pair, that would cost you fifty dollars. However, since you know they are worth $100 and you sell them for $70 a pair that is a $700 in profit just for those ten pairs of jeans. You can do this with any item.

Online Stocks

A share is a tiny piece of a business or company. Those who want to invest are able to purchase stocks through online sources and make a lot of money. Keep in mind that this also will require some startup money in order to get it going. You can invest in different stocks to gain money even while you are on vacation. This has proven over time to be a great way to make decent money online.

Marketing Specialist

If you have a good handle on how to market businesses,
then you can brand yourself a marketing specialist and
help business revive themselves or establish success.
From marketing plans to running a team, you will take the
brand and run with it. Your job is to market the company so
that they can build up a good reputation, and in return
profit.

Google Adsense

Google AdSense has brought a lot of money to those who have websites and blogs. You will sign up for a free account, build a great blog or website, and then put the Google Adsense ads on your site. When people click on the ads, you will receive money. Getting the right amount of traffic to the site is crucial, so put a lot of focus on SEO.

Amazon Associates

Amazon Associates program offers you a way to sell items on your websites. You can just build a store or you can put in products inside your posts. When you sell a product, you get a percentage. Products range from:

- Toys
- Games
- Computers
- Electronics
- Beauty Products
- Tools
- Clothing
- Purses

Rakuten Linkshare

Rakuten Linkshare offers a way to receive a percentage of the sales. Just like Amazon, you can sell items on your site and earn money. From clothing to toys, they have items that will match almost any site. There are a lot of different products that you can promote. The categories of products include:

- Computers
- Office Supplies
- Fashion and Beauty Products
- Video Games
- Books
- Movies
- Household Items
- Health and Fitness Products
- Toys
- Baby Equipment

Company Referral Programs

A company referral program will offer you cash for referring people to a company. This is done in many ways from links to ads. There are many companies that offer one or more types of company referral programs. Here are the four main types of referral programs:

- Direct Referrals: This is where you direct clients or consumers to the company via speech, link, post, etc.
- Implied Referrals: This is where once you get a product or services from a person, then you will refer your friends and family to them.
- Tangible Referrals: This is product review or service review referrals. An example of this is when a company offers you a product in return for a review on your popular blog.
- Community Referrals: This is when you promote an event or mission of a non-profit company. For example, when you purchase BLANKS this week, 10 percent of the proceeds will then go to COMPANY.

Klout

You can create content on Klout and receive money from the views that you get. This is a great way to make some cash from your skills. Klout offers a good platform for marketing and for making fun money. Here are the four parts that make this possible:

- Audience Targeting: Identify groups of the influencers in the audience.
- Influencer Outreach: The influencers are then offers exclusive rewards like early access for products, VIP events, digital promotions, and more.
- Content Creation: The influencers will then share their excitement and then they will generate their earned media.
- Campaign Analytic: Receive the campaign progress, along with results report.

Etsy

Etsy is an online platform that you can use to sell items that you have made. From paintings to jewelry, you can own an online store and sell your creations. There are many people who sell handmade or even vintage products on this platform. Here are the categories that are available:

- Baby
- Children
- Gift Ideas
- Gift Cards
- Jewelry
- VIntage
- Supplies

Upwork

Upwork is a website that is matches up workers with clients. These clients hire writers, designers, and more for small to large jobs that they need. For example, they will hire eBook writers and web designers through this site. Jobs on Upwork include jobs like:

- Article Writing
- Blog Writing
- Press Releases
- eBook Writing
- Voice Overs
- Translations
- Illustrating

MTurk

MTurk is much like Upwork. Clients will express the type of job that they need, and those who are qualified can accept the job. You in turn will get paid. You are able to get money or an Amazon gift card. There are so many different types of jobs on MTurk; however, a few of the main jobs include:

- Data Entry
- Video Transcribing
- Writing
- Surveys

Podcasting

Podcasting is a great way to earn money. You can advertise companies and individuals just like a radio station. This is completely in your control and you can go from one show a month all the way up to a weekly show. It all depends on how much you would like to put into it. Types of podcasts include:

- Music
- Sports
- Politics
- Religion
- Niche

Internet Radio

Internet radio is a great way to have some fun and make some money. You can get sponsors, advertisers, and sell space for radio hosts. This is a great way to turn a hobby into a job. If you are afraid of filling up time on your station, you can reach out to like-minded people with podcasts and play them on your station. Between your content you will sell time to those who need commercial aired for your fee.

Guest Posting

Guest posting is a great way to make money. There are websites and blogs that will offer you some money to write guest posts for them to create fresh content for their viewers. Once you have built up a decent amount of traffic, you are able to guest post on like blogs. Ensure that you have put your blog link inside you post in order to drive more traffic to your site to sell products and to earn money from clickable ads.

Selling Music

If you are musically inclined, then you are able to make music and sell the rights to people for them to use for different projects. They will use it for films, commercials, and more. How this works is you create great music. Once you have finished it, you will sign up to a site and then once another person has found your music they will purchase the rights to use it. You will split the money with the site. It is a great way to have fun passive income. Here are some sites to sign up for:

- Audiojungle
- Audiomicro
- Audiosocket
- Audiosparx
- Beatpick
- Crucial Music
- Getty Images
- Jingle Punks
- iStock
- Luck Stock
- Magnatune
- Melody Loops
- Music Loops
- Music Supervisors
- Muziko
- Partners in Rhyme
- Pond5
- Premium Beat
- Productiontrax
- Pump Audio

- Revostock
- And much more!

Kickstarter

If you want to create a project that will make you money and you need startup capital, you are able to use kickstarter to raise the money. All you have to do is write about the project, and then go from there. Those who can utilize this site include:

- Musicians
- Filmmakers
- Artists
- Writers
- And more!

Online Casino

This is a very fun way to earn money. Yes, it is gambling; however, if you are good at cards, then this is a great way to get the cash flowing. You will earn money through your winnings. Once you have built up what you would like to have, then you will request payout. Make sure to look for the payout days, as the day may be different.

CashCrate

Cashcrate is a legit site that you are able to use in order to make money doing surveys. The types of surveys differ when it comes to pay. There are different types of surveys. It is a good thing to keep track of the surveys that you do in order to watch how much money you build up. Here are the types of surveys that will be offered to you:

- Daily Surveys: With these surveys, you are able to earn $.80 per survey and up. Many people make about $48 a month from these surveys.
- Targeted Surveys: These offer $1 per survey, and you have a chance to make good money with this type.

Peer to Peer Lending

Peer to peer lending can offer you a great and steady flow of cash. You will need beginning capital and a lawyer to draw up a contract that you will use for your lending. There are many people that do not like to use banks, and you will see many people who only want to borrow around one thousand to three thousand dollars. You will earn money from this from the interest.

InfoBarrel

This is a community of many writers that offer their time in creating content that is geared towards readers in order for them to educate him or herself. It can even help them to solve a problem that they have. This site promotes those who are experts in their field. They will write what they know and earn money from it. Categories include:

- Lifestyle
- Tech
- Travel
- Entertainment
- Business
- Health
- Home

Squidoo

Squidoo is a platform in which people create content to share. They make money by placing ads on their squidoo account and then they get paid for clicks. It is much like Google Adsense. You have a lot of freedom with this site. You can write about anything that you would like to write about. There are contests and rewards for writing content that performs better than others.

Hubpages

Hubpage is much like Squidoo. Although they are different platforms, you are able to make money for writing great content and getting money from the clicks on the ads that are placed on your posts. You are able to write about anything that you would like to write about. There are multiple ad programs that you can use to promote your content and earn money. There are certain elements that you need to have.

- Pictures
- Text
- Polls
- Videos

Bukisa

Bukisa is deemed a social platform in which their users produce content. It offers a simple way to share their articles and promote businesses. The categories range from money and cars, all the way up to parenting and more. There are multiple categories that you can write in including:

- Money
- Society
- Education
- Holidays
- Family
- Home
- Food
- Health
- Hobby
- Tech
- Style
- Science
- Sport

SheToldMe

This is a great site that offers different offers to their users to make money. From phone apps to surveys. This is a site for females. There are different categories for this site. There is a lot of information under each category that is utilized by their users. The categories include:

- Business
- Entertainment
- Games
- Health
- Lifestyle
- Science
- Politics
- Technology

Best Reviewer

You are able to sign up for this site and earn money by writing reviews for different products and companies. The fees for the writers fluctuate. There are many different types of products that are reviewed by those who use this site. From makeup to yoga mats, there are endless opportunities on this site for both the company and the writer.

Rate It All

Those that sign up for this site are able to get paid for rating companies and products. It is a fun way to earn money for your opinion. You will be able to rate products, services, companies, and other aspects of a business. This serves as a marketing tool for the company and is extremely valuable to them. This is why those that put time into can make a pretty penny.

UpHype

UpHype is a site in which you can do wholesale hosting. This is a great way to make some money by doing very little work. That seeking a hosting for their many different types is able to get a discounted price with you. In turn, you will see more clients and earn more money. Would you pay more for the same thing if given the choice?

Dollar3

This is one site in which you can sport your skills. There are many different jobs in which you can earn money from $3 up to $15. Much like Fiverr, Dollar3 is a site that you are able to list your skills and get paid for them. For example, if you are an article writer, you can put a post up to write a 400-word article for $4 to make some money. If you are a designer, then offer a logo for $15. No matter what you are good at, you can monetize it.

Fittytown

This site is a skill website in which you are matched up to clients needs a certain project completed. The jobs pay $50. You can even get 10 percent of referrals. You will need to sign up for a membership and go through your profile to list the skills that you have. From logo design to writing, there are many opportunities to knock out a few projects a day and say goodbye to your day job.

TenBux

TenBux is a Fiverr site. Jobs on this site are for $10 and you can offer jobs for double of what Fiverr does. Face it, you get what you pay for. Those who need a logo for their business are more inclined to pay $10 over $5 due to the fact that you will put more into your project. From designing to writing, and more; you are able to monetize on your fun skills to make your bank account grow.

Facebook Ads

You are able to use Facebook Ads to promote any business, website, or blog. If you do a great ad campaign, then you will be rolling in the dough in no time. If you are working on making money through a blog or a website, then you can drive traffic to your clickable ads to make money. If you have product that you are selling, then Facebook Ads will help consumers become aware of your product to drive sells.

Speedy Ads

Speedy Ads is a great site that offers those with blogs and websites to earn money from it. It is much like Google Adsense in a sense. However, with Speedy Ads, there are businesses looking for like blogs and websites in which they can have ads placed. This helps traffic to your blog or site, as well as help to drive sells for the company. Different ads have different prices due to their types and time increments of placement.

Just Answer

Just Answer is a website that you can sign up for and answer questions for money. Of course, if you are an expert, then it will be even easier. There are many people who think of random subjects daily. Have you ever been in a conversation where something comes up and you turn to Google? Those few minutes are wasted when all you have to do it ask this site. Those who are members are able to answer the questions those people ask.

Kgb

Kjb offers a way to make money by answering random questions. These questions are asked by those who text them in using their cell phone. This is a cell phone based platform that allows members to make money by answering the questions that people text in. This is a fast and easy way to get answers, as well as money.

Fun Advice

This is a site in which you can offer your skills to do fun projects for a price. From illustration to the art of dance, there are so many opportunities for people to be matched up with what they need. Some of the skills that are utilized for cash are:

- Cartooning
- Web Design
- Scrapbooking
- Photography
- Dane
- Crafts

And anything else you can think of.

ChaCha

ChaCha is a site that is based on providing answers to those who want them. You will be paid to answer questions for their inbound questions. From long and personal questions to short trivia questions about films, there are many questions that you can answer to earn some money. All you have to do is sign up and begin answering.

Web Answers

This is much like ChaCha. You will be paid for answering questions. Those who need or want to find something out can ask this site. In turn, those who are members are there to answers these questions for a reward. This reward, yes you guessed it, is money!

Gazelle

If you have electronics that you do not use, you can sell them on Gazelle. You can even make a small business from buying electronics from others and then reselling them on Gazelle. All you have to do is go to the site, answer a few questions, ship your electronics to Gazelle, and then they will pay you through PayPal or Amazon gift cards.

Amazon

Amazon is a great way to sell items that you want. From eBooks to real books, from toys to beauty product; the possibilities are virtually endless. There are many people who hand make items and sell it, and then there are those who purchase bulk items and resell them on Amazon. There are even writers who write eBooks to sell through Amazon.

Shopit

This is a phone app in which you can use to take a picture of an item and resell it to others that have the phone app. This is much like a hybrid of Craigslist and eBay. Those with cool items that they just do not want anymore can upload pictures and sell the items. That purse that you do not use, but is in great condition can bring you in some cash.

Sell.com

Sell.com is a site in which you can sell items to earn money. Depending on the time that you put into it will determine how much money you will make. There are many different categories that you are able to place an item under to sell. Here are some of the categories:

- Pets and Animals
- Cars and Vehicles
- Real Estate

And much more. .

Oodle

Oodle is much like Craigslist. You are able to do business with people in your own area. If you have a couch, list it. If you have a car, list it. If you are selling your mad skills, sell them. You can make money doing and selling anything that you would like.

Backpage

Backpage is also like Craigslist. You are able to use this site to sell the items that you would like to those that search this site. There are many people who purchase bulk items and then sell them through this site. There are others who offer services like tutoring and more that can sell their time.

Amazon Associates

Amazon Associates is a great program that you are able to use in order to sell items that are not yours, yet still make a percentage. You are able to sell items through your website and earn a part of the sell. Some of the items that you can use to help build your bank account are:

- Make Up
- Clothing
- Tools
- Electronics
- Purses
- Shoes

And so much more!

• Commission Junction

Commission Junction is much like Amazon Associates. However, there are many different companies that you can partner with. You will sign up for the site and then look through the companies that have joined the program. They will look through your profile and either tells you yes or no. Once you get the green light, you can browse their extensive product lines to sell through your site to get a percentage of the sells.

E-Junkie

E-Junkie offers you a way to sell your digital products. This is also a renewable product source. You will not have to remake something just to sell it. Once you are finished, you can sell it as many times as you would like too. They offer many different payment types and you will be able to build up a small business with the brand being you.

CafePress

CafePress is a way to sell your digital art for items like mugs, bags, and more. There are many people who love personalized items, and you can be part of it.

E*Trade

This is a site in which you are able to use to invest. This opens money-making opportunities when it comes to investments.